The Men's World — Yesterday and Today

The Three Attributes of the Father-Mother-God and
the Capitulation of the Satanist

The eternal word,
the One God, the Free Spirit,
speaks through Gabriele,
as through all the prophets of God —
Abraham, Job, Moses, Elijah, Isaiah,
Jesus of Nazareth,
the Christ of God

The Men's World —
Yesterday and Today

The Three Attributes
of the Father-Mother-God and
the Capitulation of the Satanist

Gabriele,
the teaching prophetess and emissary
of God in our time

Gabriele
Publishing House

*"The Men's World — Yesterday and Today
The Three Attributes of the Father-Mother-God and
the Capitulation of the Satanist"*

1st Edition August 2022
© Gabriele-Verlag Das Wort GmbH
Max-Braun-Str. 2, 97828 Marktheidenfeld
www.gabriele-verlag.com
www.gabriele-publishing-house.com

Translated from the original German title:

„Die Männerwelt – gestern und heute.
Die drei Eigenschaften des Vater-Mutter-Gottes und
die Kapitulation des Satanisten"

The German edition is the work of reference
for all questions regarding the meaning of the contents.

Order No. S194TBEN PoD

All decorative letters: © Gabriele-Verlag Das Wort

ISBN 978-3-96446-323-4

The Men's World — Yesterday and Today

The Three Attributes
of the Father-Mother-God and
the Capitulation of the Satanist

Dear fellow people, my name is Gabriele. Many people know me, Gabriele, through the many revelations of God and the spiritual books and meditations from the Spirit of God.

For almost five decades, I have been receiving the eternal word of the Eternal All-One, of His Son, the Christ of God, and of the Cherub of the third basic power of God, His eternal Wisdom. During the initial years, the Cherub of His eternal Wisdom, called Brother Emmanuel — thus named for us human beings — taught and trained me to be the prophetess of God. Since that time, the Cherub of the eternal Wisdom of God has been at my side, at the side of the prophetess of God. During this cycle of nearly five decades, the Cherub, as the teacher Brother Emanuel, also taught the path to the Kingdom of God, the Inner Path for all pupils.

During these decades, many things were revealed to me, the prophetess of God — also called the emissary of the Kingdom of God by the Eternal — of which much was merely intimated in books; an expansion or pursuance of the content was planned for a later time. This knowledge was retained in my soul by the eternal All-One. The eternal God, His Son Christ and the Cherub of divine Wisdom would reveal it when the time, that is, the years, were ripe for this. From year to year, ever more was revealed, which can now also be read and heard.

To my prophetic task, the following: Right at the beginning of the training for the prophetic word, the Cherub of eternal Wisdom revealed to me that my prophetic mission from the Kingdom of God was merely a so-called eventuality that would become effective if the male gender, which is in the divine mission to help found a people and to make provisions for a better time, fails once again — as during the past millennia.

In general, it is precisely the male gender that finds it difficult to accept the natures of the sonship and daughtership of God, the three attributes, the being in the Father-Mother-God: Kindness, Love and Meekness.

In three-dimensional words, the three attributes of God are Patience, Love and Mercy.

 explain without digression, why, precisely, a woman was trained as God's prophetess:

When some divine beings of the Kingdom of God joined together to discuss their devised systems, which deviated from the eternal law of love, the evil had already begun. The thus stirred up turmoil led them to rise up against unity and equality, against the three attributes and the duality in the Father-Mother-God. The renegade spirit beings left the Kingdom of God with a considerable quantity of Light-Ether — which, however, was merely a loan — in order to create according to their concepts. In this consciousness, they also created a wall of light before the Kingdom of God. Now, they were outside the Kingdom of God on still-disorganized light-ethereal planets.

Already at the beginning, immediately after turning away from the Eternal Kingdom, the problems began. In the process, the three attributes of God were suppressed, and the four elementary powers, the divine powers of drawing and creating of Order, Will, Wisdom and of divine Earnestness, were reversed and turned into their opposite, in order to largely exclude the three attributes of God. Soon the disputes began.

Each one wanted to be the greatest and to subordinate his kind to his own ideas. The first quarrel began. Some felt called to present and offer their regime, their devised system. Already at the beginning of the most diverse systems, the renegade beings introduced the so-called mystical numbers. Each regime, each system, now had a mystical number. The dispute over supremacy was organized by the mystical number in such a way that each regime, each system, gave itself its own mystical number. In the corresponding divine revelations, we can read about the systematic procedure of the beings of the Fall and their first Fall-systems up to the religions.

For their first reversed four powers of drawing and creating, the Fall-beings developed the respective systems and number combinations. As stated, each regime, each system, had its, still mystical, combinations of numbers, with which it drew and created from the loan, the Light-Ether, the first and the additional Fall-cosmoses that became ever denser. In this creative paroxysm of joy, the three attributes of God were hardly considered any more.

At the beginning of the Fall, the Fall-beings still had fine-material bodies. During the further course of the Fall, finer-material bodies developed, and later, with further densification, the coarse-material emerged more and more. In this process of densification, as we have heard, the mystical number combinations also emerged. Over the course of the Fall-times toward coarse-materiality, the mixture of numbers began more and more. Everything else, such as today's numerical code, is based on the mystical mixture of numbers.

The reversal of polarity of the mystical numbers by system took place soon after the Fall from the Kingdom of God. The transformation, the conversion of the Light-Ether up to the densification of the Fall-systems, the finer-material cosmoses, took place in rhythms: from Order to disorder, from the Will of God to self-will, from the Wisdom of God to the intellect, from Earnestness to indifference. With these four powers of drawing and creating, which were turned around, that is, reversed in polarity, the Fall-authorities wanted to create their own cosmoses, which they succeeded in doing to a limited extent. The three attributes of God, Patience, Love and Mercy, which are predominantly designated to the female principle, were consciously rejected.

But both, man and woman, have in themselves the seven positive forces to supplement one another, only with respectively different expressions.

Through the reversal of polarity, the change of the four powers of drawing and creating by the mystical Fall-numbers, there followed a visible turning point in the four powers of drawing and creating and relative to the three attributes of God.

The Fall divide had consequences. In the times of times into the present time, a men's world was built up, which, in itself, already bore the decay that is becoming more and more visible today, because in all of the men's world, the attributes of God, the Patience, Love and Mercy, are extremely atrophied. From this point onward, women were not only treated in a derogatory way by the men's world, but were also disdained, and depending on the country and religious order, regarded as inferior and deprived of their human rights. The change of the mystical numbers in the Fall-systems, which led to a certain male society, took its course. The male gender increasingly lost access to the principle of the female, to the three attributes of Patience, Love and Mercy.

From all the misconduct against the seven positive basic powers, the eternal law of God, aggression, dominance, monitoring others, lies and secrets developed more and more. Thereby, the woman fell below any kind of value, to the point of servitude for house and home, she was downgraded to maidservant and treated accordingly, often like a slave, humiliated by abuse and contempt, whereby the men's world increasingly positioned itself.

From Fall-generation to Fall-generation, the three divine attributes were not only neglected, but were no longer considered at all. Instead, the male gender "ennobled" itself — with the crown of hubris.

No one asked about the message of God through His emissaries, through the prophets and prophetesses. As of yore, the nation of lemmings followed after the priests and their kind — but not to ask what God, the Eternal, said through His messengers. At the time of Jesus and after His terrible murder on the cross, it continued into the present time. The people now had their alleged so-called "Christian leaders" in church and state power with their soldiers who went from country to country wrecking havoc, like the hordes of the underworld. No one asked: Where does the conflicting nature of religious doctrines come from? Does it come from the Kingdom of God, or are these the idolatrous teachings of the guild of priests of yesterday, that is, from times of yore, and that, to this day?

Because of these correlations from one cruel time to another with more cruelties, as briefly mentioned, the eventuality from the Kingdom of God took effect: the incarnation of the Seraph of divine Wisdom, in order to serve the Eternal as God's prophetess.

At the right time, through the Kingdom of God, it was also to be made known how the demonic scepter of the underworld also acts in this world and how the demon with his reason of state of the underworld tried to completely reverse the seven primordial powers of the eternal creation for his goals: If possible, he wanted to dissolve the Kingdom of God to the extent of getting to the protection of the core of being in every soul and attacking the center of Being, by reversing the polarity of the divine elemental powers.

To make this demonic intent apparent, a herald of God, an interpreter, was needed again, for the Eternal Kingdom does not have the language of human beings.

The treatises from below, the world of yesterday and today, despite further teachings from above, adhere to the rules of the demonic scepter, which the demon of the underworld determined: to direct the four powers of drawing and creating according to his standards, which means to defile, exploit and, if possible, destroy the Earth, so that his structure of lies from the beginning of the Fall and his secret are not disclosed.

The demonic scepter, the ruler of the underworld, the demon, knows no measure, for he himself reversed the polarity of the mystical numbers to achieve his goal. Since the Fall from above, from the Eternal Kingdom, the

Fall-regime, also called the Demons' State, emits its Fall-laws, which contain more and more that is terrifying.

The downward frenzy is the demonic precepts that have brought the Earth to the edge of destruction, such as, for example:

Instead of Order — everywhere disorder in fields, forests, oceans, rivers and lakes.

Instead of God's Will — self-will, abuse, immorality and greed.

Instead of Wisdom — intellect and knowledge, the basis for egoism, arrogance, being self-opinionated and destruction.

Instead of Earnestness — indifference, grandstanding, self-aggrandizement, that is, unscrupulousness.

Instead of Kindness, the same as Patience — impatience, contention, contempt, threats and disparagement.

Instead of love for God — self-love, bumptiousness, abuse of children and women, that is, egoism, which gets out of hand more each day.

Instead of Meekness, the same as Mercy — ruthlessness against people, animals and nature; hatred, envy, theft, fratricide and sororicide, also by way of the arms trade.

These are the demonic values that are getting out of hand and are also bringing the Earth, the provider for human beings, out of balance.

As far as we humans can look back: it is always the men's world and the contempt and abuse of the woman, the rape of children and the defilement of the nature kingdoms — and none of the people and of the state apparatus ask why this is so.

The priests of the religions also do not ask why idolatry at all — when, after all, God, the Eternal, and His Son, the Christ of God, taught otherwise.

This world, the satanic ulcer of yesterday, has now reached its correspondingly low point, which has slipped into the demonic intermediate realm and has become one with the demonic delirium to destroy everything, if possible, also the planets that might still be reached. 4000 years ago and during the 4000 years since Abraham up to Gabriele, the majority of people listened and still listen to the puppet master, the idol from below, to the demonic scepter, the demon.

To think about: Who ordered, supported and executed the demonic vibration, the murder and manslaughter?

Who blessed and condoned the weapons of yesterday and today? Who was and is it, right up to the present time?

Who was and who is instrumental in the divide of killing countless animals? Who torments and kills them to this day, and who gives the order for this, and who gives the blessing for this curse over animal barns and transports, over animal testing facilities, slaughterhouses and not lastly, over the animals in the woods and fields and in the waters?

Who is pleased with the menu, which offers the appropriately prepared animal meat, and who also has the culinary delight and lust of the palate for this?

Who advocates and subsidizes the experiments to have human organs grow in animals, of course, in the name of science and in an institute that is often subsidized with taxpayers' money?

Who supports the cultivation of human tissue and organs in nutrient solutions and incubators?

Who inspires and promotes the manipulation of the DNA, genomes and organs of human beings and animals?

Who permits and initiates the removal of organs, which always originate exclusively from living people, who are, however, artificially declared dead by a formal legal declaration of death, which is diametric to all conventional criteria for a natural human death, as all medical students still learn by law today?

And what about the person's immortal soul, which experiences the evisceration of its body?

Of general interest: Who eviscerates human beings and animals? Predominantly men or women? What about when causality sets in for all those involved, according to the law: What a person sows, they will reap. One asks — who answers?

There would be quite different answers to this!

Because these turn out to be so varied, I, Gabriele, will try to ask further questions for the sake of clarification:

Did Jesus of Nazareth encourage and arrange for such things?

Did Jesus of Nazareth teach animal murder, organ transplantation, organ cultivation in animals, etc., and give instructions in this regard?

Did Jesus of Nazareth instigate wars and recommend the arms trade for the purpose of fratricide?

Did Jesus of Nazareth disregard the Ten Commandments of God through Moses, perhaps even invalidate them?

Jesus of Nazareth taught the foundation for a moral life, the Ten Commandments of God and the Sermon on the Mount. Who rendered His teachings invalid? Where do all the murderous instructions come from, and who received them yesterday and today?

Who were and are the advocates of this unscrupulous attitude, and who has participated at all times?

As far as we can look back: always the men's world.

Why mostly the male gender?

Jesus of Nazareth spoke of the "father from below," who was a liar and murderer from the beginning. Jesus taught the law of love for God and neighbor, which includes the three attributes of Kindness, Love and Meekness. Who was it that created a territory in this world without considering the three attributes of God? Who was the agitator and the leader of the destruction of the Earth, its countless resources and natural springs for humankind?

By whom and by what was the climate change initiated, and who are the victims? Who has earned and continues to earn from this the immense riches of this world, and who worships whom for them? Who has the profit from all this?

Who has "omnicide" on their plan, or has someone lost control?

As far as we can look back: always the men's world. And the contempt and abuse of women? At all times, the men's world — always, only against human beings, animals and nature, causing only suffering and misery. Are there biological or even psychiatric explanations for this disease?

Questions after questions.

Why, in His final reckoning with the demonic goings-on, does God, the Eternal, reveal the victory of the Kingdom of God over the darkness, and that the innumerable, unatoned causes will rise, country by country, city by city, in every town and at every village?

Why do God, the Eternal, His Son and the Cherub of eternal Wisdom, the one responsible in the work of the Christ of God, speak of the homebringing, that is, of the leading home into the Kingdom of God, and of victory?

As we know, victory is always preceded by capitulation!

Until the present time, the demon, the Satanist of the underworld, of the demonic state, pulled his strings in this world. From the intermediate realms came the instructions to his instruments on Earth, which then acted accordingly.

I deliberately label the demon the Satanist — and why?

Because from the very beginning and up to the present time, he took advantage of the original concern of a spiritual woman, called Satana, as a pretext and a means to an end for his devised treatises, in order to subordinate his demonic will and striving to his secret.

From the Fall-disaster on to the present time, the lie was his secret. Time moves forward, and very gradually it is revealed.

In several divine revelations, we heard again and again about the end times. Now, almost everyone realizes that the world of today, with its abominable atrocities, is no better than the world of yesterday.

An egotistically shaped society, in which primarily men are the leaders in the religions and in the economic and state powers, demonstrates the state of deepest ethical-moral degeneration all over the world. The Cherub of divine Wisdom expressed the full extent of male arrogance with the following words:

"Nothing proved — only destroyed!"

The cruel perversions that are so succinctly called the "abuse" of children and women hardly have anymore limits, just as little as the brutal destruction of the entire planet Earth. The contents of the term "men's world" were unlimited in an absolutely and completely negative sense, during the centuries and into the present time. The rage of destruction and the hubris of yesterday are the rage of destruction and the hubris of today.

They are the satanic signs of the continued descent and decline into the darkest future times and of the complete devastation of the Earth.

If one considers the full extent of the destruction of the Earth of today compared to past millennia, then every word, every expression is too weak, too harmless, as far as this thoroughly satanically shaped men's world is concerned and the state of this planet Earth.

The degenerated men's world, the vibration of yesterday is the pendulum swing of today.

During nearly five decades, I have been able to watch the pendulum of the men's world from a distance and with a certain composure: the indifference, falsehood, cowardice, selfishness and the "loners," but also the perfidious impertinence, the ruthlessness, aggressiveness and brutality — unless a woman stimulates the personal craving to be pleasing and the male compulsion to conquer her. This is easy for many a man, since many women are also already afflicted by the desire of conquest. On the one hand, one can understand this, because the woman is still searching to conquer the supposedly strong hero who stands at her side. On the other hand, the men's world simply is dominant in this world and is still the "globe" around which everything should revolve. As far as we can look back: always the men's world and the contempt and abuse of the woman.

The woman of today endeavors to emulate the male pose instead of mastering herself as the woman — without the seeming hero at her side, the male type of yesterday and today. In the eagerness to also "be worth something," the woman often acquires masculine facial features and behavior patterns that are typical of those who think they have to conquer this world.

For almost five decades, I had the opportunity at home and abroad to take a closer look at the men's world. The Eternal asked the male gender — as at all times — to preserve the Earth and to help build up what the Kingdom of God wanted to give the planet Earth in terms of help and support. It was always about the seven powers of God, primarily about the three attributes of Patience, Love and Mercy.

In all the years during which I traveled a lot, I learned to weigh and measure the differences from man to man. One had more understanding for his neighbor, also in terms of the female gender, the other noticeably signaled his dominance and his being self-opinionated many times over. From this indifferent and brutal men's world, every now and then brothers crystallized who are closer to the three attributes. The appreciation of one's neighbor made this clear. In almost five decades as prophetess and emissary of the Eternal Kingdom, I have experienced many things and learned many things from the Kingdom of God, which are now becoming evident during this time.

As already mentioned, nearly five decades ago I accepted the prophetic word, among other things, in order to call those from the male gender who are in the mission of the Kingdom of God, from the lineage of David and from other lineages, to take on what they had promised. The "Yes" to the Eternal was spoken only conditionally. The so-called manhood of all times is active and works only with the possibilities that this world offers it, without heeding the spiritual principles of life, the Ten Commandments of God through Moses and the teachings of Jesus of Nazareth, which, by being fulfilled step by step, would have offered humankind a better world.

It was nothing abstract that God, the Eternal, offered to some of His sons from the Kingdom of God. It was primarily a matter of keeping order in life, of grasping and accepting the Will of God and of reducing the self-will, the ego-centricity, and of not exalting the intellect, but of attaining Wisdom, in order to fulfill with Earnestness the work of the deed in the Will of God, and this, with Patience, Love and Mercy, which is the measure of the right deed.

That would have been the life for a better world and for healthier people.

As stated, the offer from the eternal Kingdom of God was never abstract.

It was always about the Christian values that Jesus of Nazareth taught us, the Ten Commandments of God through Moses and the steps in His Sermon on the Mount. In spite of the many teachings and aids from the Eternal Kingdom, the "Yes" to the Eternal became a "No." Both the male and female genders found it difficult when it came to the love for God and neighbor that Jesus of Nazareth taught us. Unfortunately, as so often in the times from generation to generation, one began to live what is common to all the times in the world — one served and serve oneself and one another to this day. In the wake of these emotional acrobatics inspired by the "father from below," the most varied conversations began in many families and companies about higher values and who is right.

Everyone thought they knew better. Before the women, indifference was sacrificed and the corresponding male pose was taken up, whereby jealousy among the female gender was not lacking. Which one is sought out more than the other? Those who were not so much sought out by the male gender asked the mirror: "Mirror, mirror on the wall, am I not beautiful enough in this gown?" The facet cut, an illusion from A to Z, the mirror, surely had the appropriate answer.

The Eternal, who is the unity in the law of the seven primordial powers, tried, for example, with Abraham, Moses, and other emissaries of God up to Gabriele, to build a community, which should demonstrate an ethical moral life with higher values among one another, according to the law of the love for God and neighbor. Thus, during the four thousand years, there were always the first beginnings of corresponding communities over and over again, but it did not take long, and then many of these communities disintegrated, or they were broken by the "father from below."

During the nearly five decades, in which the Cherub of the third basic power of God has stood at the side of the prophetess of God, the direct eternal word has revealed itself, which also allowed me to behold the make-up of the Eternal Kingdom and how the divine beings live and work together — and what will befall this world.

But during the nearly five decades, I have also seen the decline of a society filled with egomania and abnormalities, the extent of which is increasing all over the world.

Today, more and more people are becoming aware of the demise of this world. Without consideration of the destruction of the planet Earth, the greed and exploitation of people, nature and animals have already become the order of the day, people help themselves, whatever the cost.

This world sacrifices itself, because since the Fall-drama up to the present day, people listen to the church gods or believe in no God, because they do not want the cruel church god. Some people say: "The eternal All-One God spoke His last word through the prophets of times long past, and now He is silent."

This is an ecclesiastical belief, to which also the state power has been and continues to be in bondage at all times. But for thousands of years, and continuously, the eternal Father, the Father-Mother-God who is the Love, sent His messengers, His prophets and prophetesses to the Earth in an uninterrupted stream of love from the Kingdom of God.

Everything reaches its high point one time. The time of over 4000 years is coming to an end. The Eternal, who addressed His word over and over again to the people of all generations through His prophets and prophetesses, also 2000 years ago through His Son, the Christ of God, is now taking back the energy, the Light-Ether, the loan, to the destructive Fall-society, which will have tangible effects for humankind and the Earth. HE, the Eternal, has directed the final word to humankind concerning the dissolution of the system "Fall."

We can also speak of a so-called end-time revelation, because the Earth, the provider for humankind, can no longer support the degenerated human race of exploitation and destruction.

The disaster of yesterday is now coming to an end in the victory of the Kingdom of God against the Fall-regime of the underworld and thus, against the Demons' State and its ruler, the Satanist.

With appropriate emphasis I, Gabriele, call him the Satanist because he did not want to reveal his secret.

After a certain stretch of the way in the Fall-event, the female being, Satana, had stopped following the Satanist. She began to see through the Satanist's plan, his true intentions, namely, to pursue the dissolution of the Eternal Kingdom.

On the downward path of domination and in the desire to defeat the Eternal Kingdom, the so-called Demons' State built up its guild of domination.

The supreme commander of this state wanted to force the female being, Satana, to show solidarity with him and disclose to him the details, the correlations about the erection, that is, the creation, of the Eternal Kingdom. Through this blackmail of the female principle Satana, the Satanist once again wanted to try and attack the course of creation of the Eternal Kingdom. As once before, the female principle, Satana, refused to heed the Satanist.

In spite of everything, the reversed mystical number remained his secret, the hatred against the woman. The Kingdom of God has so far been silent about this purpose of the vassals, for there was more to come.

In the Christ-revelation *This is My Word, Alpha & Omega,* the liberation of the so-called woman, Satana, was briefly revealed by Christ Himself.

The struggle for the justice of God, the All-Law, God, is not lost. God, the Eternal, has the answer for every soul and every human being. No being is lost, not even if it violates the basic principles of life, the unity. The eternal law is in every soul, in every ensouled human being. Nothing and no one can become totally and completely lost, because the eternal law is unity, it is God's love, and God, the All-Law, is the love and the love of neighbor.

God, the Creator of all Being, is the Father-Mother-God, who fights for every created being, no matter how small and insignificant it may seem to us human beings. Even if soul beings and ensouled human beings currently want it differently than the All-Law, God is love and love of neighbor. Because it is so, as stated, neither soul nor human being is lost. The same applies to the being, Satana, and the Satanist, about which we will still hear and read.

Everything has its time, and in time, its high point, to allow that to become evident, for which, apparently, it is now time to become manifest. As the morning brings forth the day, so does the secret also come to light.

Countless times have passed during which a son from the Sanctum wanted to blackmail the female being, Satana, to explain to him the knowledge of the structuring of creation and all the details concerning the spiritual fusion of the seven seas of light and how the principle of creation is apportioned and how the whole course of creation takes place, and more. The female being, the woman Satana, is a being from the primordial creation and therefore, has insight into the "Let there be."

The dissolution of creation was never the goal of the female principle, Satana. She wanted to achieve absoluteness in the three attributes of the Father-Mother-Being.

The ruler of the demonic state took advantage of this desire for his goals. Because Satana did not follow him, to this day, he has fought against the female principle, the woman, and labelled Satana with the name "Satan." In the times of the further Fall from the Kingdom of God to the further densifications of the Fall-cosmoses and of the former divine beings, the hatred of the Satanist against the woman became ever greater. When he recognized the further consequences for the former divine beings — of which he is also one — he soon entered the opposite into the mystical number. His concern was directed against the spiritual woman from the Sanctum.

The consequence of this was that the numerical component of the male part changed faster than he thought. The quarreling and strife in this one-sided reversal of polarity began already before the density of matter.

Now I once again draw a great arc to matter. Once divine, fine-material beings became beings of a finer-material kind, then the density of the beings followed more and more, which increased ever more, becoming coarse-materiality, that is, human beings. As far back as we can think, we know about the human race. It developed over countless ages, since the Fall of the divine beings from the Kingdom of God.

A brief repetition:
With the change of the mystical number, the declaration of war against the neighbor already began. In the continuing transformation toward density, toward matter, the fighting against others continued.

The man in the battle format of the human being continued to draw his sword, despite the many heralds of God who brought the eternal word to the people, who admonished and taught the path to peace.

Fighting and murder continued; people and animals were killed; men, women and children were not only imprisoned in dungeons, but tortured and tormented in every conceivable way, and women and girls were raped in great numbers. To this day, the sexual abuse of children, thus, child abuse, and the abuse of women are the order of the day, also in so-called civilized, allegedly Christian countries. To this day, the man is dominant in this disastrous world.

Shortly after the Fall from the Eternal Kingdom, the mystical number was changed to such an extent that it had a decisive impact on the giving part — spoken today: the male part, the male gender.

Summarized for our time, this means: the mix of numbers, the numerical code, the DNA. Now, everything is based on numbers, numbers, numbers, the numerical code — DNA.

As explained in a divine revelation, the four powers of drawing and creating and the three attributes of God, the filiation attributes, are the principle of life of all divine beings, the sonship and daughtership of God. The principle of life of the All-Unity also includes the principle of duality, from which the divine families emerge. The eternal law of God is the principle of life of the divine beings, the sons and daughters of God. It is the principle of equality in the duality. The female principle, Satana, also affirmed this and lived accordingly, but the aspiration of her desires and wanting remained: to be more than what the configuration of the eternal law contains, equality in the duality.

Thus, in the eternal law there is no inequality between the male and the female principle. There is also no momentary being in love and tomorrow, again differently. God is love, and everything is balanced in the love for God and neighbor in all the details of the Being.

Thus, the eternal love is the balanced principle of life, also in duality, the Being in the Being, eternally. Love in God also includes freedom and unrestricted movement in all of infinity. Thus, there is no restriction, no demarcation to the neighbor, the so-called "other one," and no rating that is directed "upward" or "downward." This also determines equality in the eternal law, and thus, justice.

In the eternal law, God, there is neither requesting nor giving thanks. The eternal universal All-law of infinity is the All-communication, sending and receiving. The unity in the law, God, are the divine beings, images of the Father-Mother-Being.

There have often been reports about the Fall-realm and its experts. What should be known and what is important can be read in the divine revelations that have been given.

The mix of numbers has its effect. The animal and plant worlds, as well, everything that bears life on Earth, is programmed with the number of hatred against the female and thus, oriented toward "eradication."

Over the course of time, a men's world increasingly crystallized, which continuously weakened its degenerated consciousness by fighting against the neighbor, against the female and continued every kind of abuse, also against the animal and plant worlds.

As far as we can look back: always the men's world and the contempt and abuse of the woman.

What became of the male gender over time? A despot, an aggressive, ready to fight type, who is against women. If his posturing does not produce the desired result, all appreciation is lost, also in relation to Mother Earth with her unimaginable, manifold resources and living beings.

The secret "against the woman" and the further campaigns of eradication of the messengers of God caused the degeneracy of the man and the hubris of the men's world, also when it involves going against the life of the animal and plant worlds, ultimately, against the entire planet Earth. Through the word of revelation from the Kingdom of God, we know today that changes in the chromosomes are not by chance, they are not a coincidental step of evolution, but conscious inputs into the mystical numbers.

In nature there is no coincidental evolutionary leap or "nature just made it that way." In all of infinity there are no coincidences. The deformity of the man's Y-chromosome was preceded by an act of will of the once high spirit being, who, by reversing the polarity of the four basic powers of God and by rejecting the three filiation attributes of God, called Patience, Love and Mercy on Earth, influenced the DNA of men via the mystical numbers, with the following result: Polarity reversal up to the deformed Y-chromosome, which continues to degenerate, as biologists impressively demonstrate in scientific studies.

With the Satanist's campaign of revenge against the female principle, based on the atomic structure of the numbers mixture all the way to the DNA, he ultimately harmed himself, because he increasingly lost the comprehensive view. The deception of the Satanist and the other Fall-experts against the woman, the spiritual female being, also concerning the word of the Eternal about the heralds of God, thus had far-reaching consequences. Soon after the Fall from the Eternal Kingdom, the woman Satana remained behind, but the word "Satan" is still the emotive word to this day.

The woman — "Satana" — was now called Satan and up to the present time is decried as the "devil."

But the demonic ruler, who until now has fought the three divine attributes of Kindness, Love and Meekness, is male. His secret is the number, and the DNA in the numerical code.

To understand the correlations: Because the inverted, that is, the reversed polarity of the number became the superior existence, about 2000 years ago, the Co-Regent of the Kingdom of God intervened and released a part of His divine heritage, to protect the core of being, the essence of the Kingdom of God, in all souls and ensouled human beings, because the inequality between man and woman was heading toward a precedent-setting, dangerous and destructive goal.

Despite the "It is finished" of Jesus, the Christ, on the cross of agony, the lie and the secret continued. With the lie, and under the abuse of the name "Christ," that is, "Christian," the Satanist continued his campaign against the primordial creation, against the Eternal Kingdom of God.

And being as it is: The Eternal continued to send His messengers.

Once the Satanist believed that the Eternal would not offer any resistance, he continued to use the dictum of Satana under the name "Satan," which was well received in the religions of this world, because the lie and the secret became the foundation of sand in ecclesiastical usage. Because this attraction, the secret of the religious leaders, was accepted as God's Will by the state and the people, the agent of dark authority believed this would now be his victory.

Once again, I, Gabriele, draw a great arc to today's world and to the planet Earth, which became the territory of human beings and which humankind sees as its home planet. Ever since we have been able to look back, the institutional rulers have shaped the climate of war and manslaughter, murder and much more. God, the Eternal, was further downgraded to a tin god by church and state organs, without considering what Jesus of Nazareth had taught and exemplified.

With the belief of the people in the tin gods of the religions and with the brutal and violent pressure over centuries on the people to believe, initiated and carried out by the guild of priests, the knowledge of the Eternal Kingdom and of its messengers was temporarily suppressed to the greatest extent, but not completely. Over the centuries, many people — not to say the majority — were mercilessly forced to be "either dead or Catholic," to which countless people reacted lethargically with church faith or indifference, when it concerned believing in a soul or even in a God from above, in the Kingdom of God.

The majority of people seem to be left to their own devices, or they remain outwardly faithful to religion, so as to still adhere to something or other that might supposedly look like it was "willed by God."

Since Moses, the Golden Calf erected by priests and the people has stood for worship. As if nothing had happened, as if there were no Resurrected One, the people elects its leaders from generation to generation, from whom it hopes they will bring the manna, the Golden Calf of ancient times and the hoped-for abundance.

The majority of people have lost faith in the true, speaking God and in His guidance, for the word of God through the mouth of a prophet was driven from people's lives by the sacrificial blood cult of the priests of the demonic tin god of religions and under threat of torture and murder. This chapter would have many pages, in order to uncover the deception, which became a lie and a secret.

Without any scruples in relation to the teachings of Jesus of Nazareth, until today, the guild of priests, the leaders of the religions and of the powerful in the state, still appropriate the name of Jesus of Nazareth.

Jesus of Nazareth taught the people to live according to the Ten Commandments of God through Moses and according to the Sermon on the Mount.

What became of the Ten Commandments of God? What became of the Sermon on the Mount? They were obscured and distorted, disparaged as untopian ideals that could not be lived — thus, one single lie! Where does the lie come from, and who followed and follows it?

The crucifix, too, the cross with corpus, openly depicts the lie, and, for nearly 2000 years, has been celebrated and worshiped as an instrument of torture and as the dominance of the lie, and abused for many a cruel purpose, and this, under the designation of "Christian values."

As far as we can look back: always the men's world, and in it, the guild of priests and the contempt and abuse of the woman.

Until now, no one has questioned how the lie that became a secret came into being, although this degenerated world has been showing signs of it for thousands of years.

The word of revelation from the Eternal Kingdom contained general admonitions and divine teachings about the entity, Satana, but no details, not about the ruler of the Demons' State and his followers either. The Demons' State was merely reported about in general terms, so as not to reveal something that had not yet reached its time.

That is simply the law of the Eternal Kingdom, the love for God and neighbor. It betrays no being, not even if this being comes from the center of the Kingdom of God, not even if this being uses other beings from the Kingdom of God to build up and expand its conspiratorial goals against the Eternal Kingdom.

As stated, everything has its time. Some time ago, the following took place, which is only now becoming apparent: The Satanist, the ruler and commander of the Demons' State, threw his signet, his coat of arms, the sign of his leadership, that is, influence, onto the Earth and deserted his satanic, that is, demonic, reason of state, which

50

means that he left the protection of his conditions of existence, the preservation and expansion of the power of the Demons' State.

As far back as we humans can orient ourselves into the past and reconstruct the devastation over the millennia, there was always only conflict and strife, person against person, nations against nations, conflict on a small scale, in families, at work and not least, in the world of human thoughts — conflict and war at all times.

Who were and are the so-called heroes of the nations? Men, men, men, and again men.

Where did the orders come from, and who blessed the march against the neighbor?

As far back as we can orient ourselves, the blessings for this came under the scepter of eradication of the priests and their servile vassals. For 2000 years they have been coming and come from church leaders, from emperors and kings; and today, from the powerful in the state, and this, to the disgrace of so-called

Christianity, mostly from so-called "Christian" countries under the designation of "Christian values."

The hidden scepter of lies of four millennia is enveloped with the long-known word "secret" or mystery.

Who carries the scepter of secrets and who constantly keeps "the mystery" on his tongue? When it comes to not having to answer precarious questions extensively, one thinks, without saying it, of the Church leaders who have "the mystery of God" as a disguise in their preacher's pocket. What is the name of the god who wanted to keep his secret, no matter who had to pay for it?

In all the spectacle of the world, once again, the men's world is the highest authority. In our time, some women are also allowed to raise their voices. Why is this possible?

Upon closer inspection, we realize that the male gender is getting weaker and weaker. This means that the DNA increasingly reveals the deformity of the man.

The whole religious disaster around the alleged "mystery of God" should neither be derided nor underestimated, if one considers the commitment of countless prophets and prophetesses and places whole communities and peoples into the scale-pan. Who contributes to the counterweight?

The men's world of all generations, including the men's society of the theological guild in churches and state organs.

For over four thousand years, the God of Abraham, Isaac and Jacob has sent His divine heralds, the admonishers and divine teachers, who brought and bring the commandment of life to the people in all the nations of the Earth: the true God of love for God and neighbor, particularly in the three attributes of God: Patience, God's Love for all life, and Mercy for people and animals. Precisely the three attributes of the true God have not been heeded since time immemorial and have increasingly been invalidated.

Who was it until the present time?

Who had many heralds of God murdered and who exterminated the early Christian communities? Is it the lie that became a secret? Who was the emitter under the lie that became a secret and who is the receiver? Who was, and is, in alliance with the lie and the secret?

Why did God, the Eternal, the Eternal Kingdom, unceasingly send an uninterrupted stream of God's heralds who gave revelations that were different from what the bearers of secrets of the religions preached, and still preach?

Who had the heralds of God persecuted and murdered? Who ordered and carried out the command to eradicate, the bloody battles and slaughter of the early Christian communities, of children, women, men, of old and sick people?

Who was it, and who is it still today, when it is about keeping the divine-prophetic word of the present time under wraps and to silence it? The men's world under the flag, "religion."

Why did the eternal All-One God send His faithful ones again and again? At all times, His concern was that primarily the men, the Sons of God, understand and accept the life principle of unity, for instance, the equality of man and woman, for the principle of equality is contained in the three attributes of the Kingdom of God. It is the dual principle of Meekness, of Love and Kindness, which is also contained in the four powers of drawing and creating — Order, Will, Wisdom and Earnestness.

Figuratively speaking, this means to bring the mystical number — once reversed in its polarity by the Satanist and anchored today in the DNA — into balance again, that is:

– instead of disorder, to come into divine Order;

– to transform self-will into the divine Will, whereby the proportionate balance is always the law of love for God and neighbor;

– instead of accumulating intellectual knowledge, to attain divine Wisdom, the right work of the deed for a moral life;

– instead of indifference and egocentricity, Earnestness in a correct way of thinking, speaking and acting.

That would be the character of the man and, of course, also of the woman.

This results in unity and a spirit of community, the commandment of love for neighbor, also in terms of the animal world and toward all of Mother Earth, which is the provider for humankind.

That was solely what the Eternal wanted and wants. With this reversal of the mystical number, the man would have become the giving principle and the woman, the receiving principle. From this, would have gradually developed unity and life, insight and peace.

Many a one is thinking: "That would be nice!"

The "would be" is now becoming fact.

The negativity in this world has reached its high point.

We continue reading what the end and the final accounting of this world will bring:

After the Satanist had in vain exhausted all his possibilities to defeat the Kingdom of God, and before his impotence became visible in the demonic state divide of his loyal followers, he deserted and wandered around in the lower causal planes, from one demonic state region to the other. His state authorities, who tracked him down, tried to bring him to reason, but they couldn't.

The Kingdom of God, which has everything under control via the All-Law, watched these blackout spells of the deserter, the leader of the Demons' State.

Soon afterward, the first signals arrived at the Sanctum of the Kingdom of God, the first signs of his intention. At the same time, he asked for an escort, in order to present his proposal in the Sanctum, the center of the Kingdom of God.

Immediately, the cherubim of the seven basic powers of God appeared and provided him safe-conduct. Arriving at the Sanctum of God, he stood before the Regent of the third basic power of God, the eternal Wisdom.

As the Satanist looked around where he was, which had once been his spiritual homeland, the process of handing over his scepter began, his surrender of demonic power. As a sign of his capitulation — without pros and cons — he handed over to the Regent of the third basic power of God his scepter of power, that is, of the leadership of the Demons' State.

All the divine beings of the infinite Eternal Kingdom experienced the high point of capitulation. The bane of the lie, which became a secret, the "for and against" that clung to the demonic scepter, was weighed and now falls under the law of expiation — for the Fall-minters who, despite knowing better, listened to the satanic goings-on, in order to portray themselves to the people as the heroes of the people, as well as for the leaders in science, economy, church and state power.

The agenda of the many deliberate and still unatoned deceptions and crimes, the excesses triggered by the church and state organs of all times, the abuse of the name of Jesus, the Christ, all that is unatoned and that could have been remedied with the teachings of Jesus of Nazareth, and, in the present time, with the many teachings, schoolings and not least, the many divine revelations directly from the Kingdom of God — everything that is unatoned in this respect — the Eternal Kingdom has handed over to the cortege of horror, about which the Eternal gave a revelation in His final accounting. Everything is measured and weighed. Neither the church leaders nor the state organs, nor the people, can avoid the scales, the law of cause and effect, in future times.

Who was it, and who are the indifferent ones and the opponents of the eternal word of the heralds of God? Who preferred superstition, the illusions of the power experts to the word of God?

Who let the guild of priests prevail, also in terms of the terrible Way of the Cross and the death of agony of Jesus of Nazareth?

Who is still indifferent to the teachings of Jesus of Nazareth today?

Everything is weighed and measured and assigned to the cortege of horror, the unatoned causes.

Starting with the year 2019, it was generally reported in divine revelations. The prophetess of God, the interpreter of the Kingdom of God, was and is merely the instrument, through which the victory of the Kingdom of God was made manifest.

It is finished.
It is accomplished.
It is done.

It is finished:

Two thousand years are gradually coming to an end, during which the name of Jesus of Nazareth was abused. The Co-Regent of the Kingdom of God in Jesus of Nazareth released a part of His divine heritage and protected the core of being in all souls and ensouled human beings. It is the essence of the Kingdom of God.

It is finished. Since Jesus of Nazareth, the heralds of God have come again and again. From the very center of the Being, came the Wisdom of God, the Seraph, and with her, many brothers and sisters to accompany her and, with the Cherub of eternal Wisdom who worked from the Kingdom of God, to support the woman. Everything is measured and weighed and justly apportioned to souls and human beings.

As the Eternal revealed: The cortege of horror, the cortege of causality, is gaining momentum.

It is finished. It is accomplished. It is done.

The victory of the Kingdom of God, of the Eternal Kingdom, was made known in the divine revelations starting at the beginning of 2019 — and now, also the capitulation of the demon, the commander of the state of the underworld.

Thus, the demon of the Fall-system has capitulated.

As after every war in this world, when the defeated ruler, the commander, has long since admitted defeat, the former instructions of the commander, the reason of state of the underworld, have not yet dried up. We are now experiencing this on Earth. The demonic regime continues to fight for power, which, of itself, will dissolve more and more.

According to the Will of the Eternal All-One, I, Gabriele, the prophetess of God, took on the eventuality of the divine prophetic word, in order to once again admonish humankind and to move it to turn back, to understand the acrobatics of numbers in time — but humankind remained as it was four thousand years ago.

Through the victory of the Eternal Kingdom, the divine prophetic word that the Eternal God entrusted to me, Gabriele, now goes back to God, the Eternal, as it is His Will. The message from the Kingdom of God, the emissary of God, named Gabriele, still remains on the Earth to receive instructions from the Eternal Kingdom. This is what the Eternal wants. His will is done.

The homebringing of souls and ensouled human beings is now an essential task of the third basic power before God's throne, the divine Wisdom. It is carried out in absolute accord with the Co-Regent of the Kingdom of God, once in Jesus of Nazareth.

he Earth heard the call of the Eternal: a new heaven and a new Earth.

On the Earth, however, it is far from over with the Fall-disaster and the sinful human race. According to the law of transformation of the Fall-cosmoses, the Earth indeed gets a new garment, but the transformation of the Fall-cosmoses and of the material cosmos takes place from above, from the first immediate Fall-cosmos after the wall of light. From above, from the Kingdom of God, from the first finer-material Fall-cosmos, the restructuring takes its course.

During this powerful transformation, by way of the restructuring, many changes are taking place. For example, the paths of souls lead only upward, back into the Kingdom of God. Even if it will take ever so long until the wall of light completely dissolves through the expiation and cleansing of the shadows on the souls and in their soul particles — the pathways from puri-fication plane to purification plane lead upward.

Every soul that wants to return to Earth will be led to the wheel of reincarnations. On the other hand, souls that have consciously violated the indications and teachings from the Kingdom of God and consciously left undone the last cycle of the past four thousand years — that in this high time of the teachings from the divine Wisdom, have thrown down the gauntlet before the Eternal, against His word and His works — will still seek out the wheel of reincarnations much more often, returning to the Earth again and again.

During the course of transformation, there will be Earth-spots, in order to come back again or even more often as human beings.

Very gradually, the Earth will become a place of expiation for some time and for working off the shadows on the soul and in the soul particles. But the word of the Eternal All-One God takes its course: a new heaven and a new Earth.

The new heaven, of which the Eternal revealed, begins with the change of the wall of light.

Up to now, a soul that had worked its way forward and reached the four planes of development to the Kingdom of God, in order to prepare for the further steps into the Kingdom of God, first had to learn how to overcome the back-radiation into the purification planes before the wall of light that had been set up by the Fall-system.

The Fall-system had created an energetic mirror system around the wall of light, which, through the back-radiation of the Fall-system, was supposed to cause the souls to turn away from the wall of light. Often, the result was that many a soul thought that the planes of preparation to the Kingdom of God were already the Kingdom of God, because through the back-radiation, that is, the counter-radiation of reflection of the wall of light, many turned back, thinking that it did not go any further.

The view into the Eternal Kingdom was thus denied to the souls by the counter-radiation and persuaded them that they were already in heaven, in the Kingdom of God. That is why the divine beings repeatedly came from the Kingdom of God to school the souls and to teach the principles of the law on how they can overcome the counter-radiation.

That, too, is now over. Seen from the Kingdom of God, the wall of light is becoming brighter and more translucent to the extent that souls in the preparation planes and in the upper purification planes can look into the Kingdom of God and see their homeland shining. This causes the souls to light up, an incentive to clear up what still needs to be cleared up. This joy flows throughout all the lower cosmoses, in which souls live and go their ways.

The jubilation of the brothers and sisters in the Kingdom of God about the victory over the Fall-system can be heard in all the Fall-cosmoses. The souls in the wheel of reincarnations also share in it and strive to make use of their coming incarnation.

All in all, this contributes to undertaking the transformation, the change by radiation of the first Fall-cosmos after the wall of light — it is the first finer-material cosmos, that is, it is not a fine-material cosmos.

How does the transformation take place? Starting from the first finer-material Fall-Cosmos after the wall of light, the gravitation of the planets changes. With the irradiation of the primordial central power, of the Light-Ether, by way of the ethereal prism suns, the suns in the finer-material cosmos are irradiated; this changes the gravitation. The respective sun gradually draws its planets to itself. With the irradiation of the primordial principle of the primordial power, of the Light-Ether, the luminous intensity of the energetic sun increases, as does its rotation. With this, the position of the sun with the planets assigned to it also changes in relation to the Kingdom of God. One could say that it moves toward the eternal homeland, toward the primordial power. With the slow and careful irradiation of the primordial power of the Light-Ether, it moves in ever more light-filled pathways toward the primordial power, also called the Primordial Central Star. According to the rhythm of the eon, to which the light intensity belongs, it is gradually absorbed by the Central Star, by the Light-Ether, and led to the corresponding eon.

Spoken with three-dimensional words: In this way, the change by radiation, the transformation, takes place from "above," from the Eternal Kingdom. This takes place in all cosmoses outside the so-called wall of light.

The resonances of the transformation from "above" are perceived in all finer-material cosmoses, as well as in the material universe and on the Earth, in the world, and have corresponding effects. This, as an explanation given for understanding the words of the Eternal All-One: a new heaven and a new Earth.

The cosmic transformation of the Fall-cosmoses from the finer-material all the way to matter, thus takes place from the Kingdom of God. Depending on the density of the solar systems, it goes faster or slower, but the primordial radiation of transformation always emanates from the center of the Kingdom of God, from the primordial power.

The primordial system, the Central Star with its prism suns, carries out the transformation of all planetary systems, both in the finer-material cosmoses, as well as in the coarse-material universe. With this, all souls are considered that are in certain purification planes and also all those that move on the "roadways" toward the Kingdom of God. The wheel of reincarnations also gets the appropriate attention.

Because this is so, the solar systems in the lower planes receive special attention, above all, in the material cosmos. The material cosmos is an exception, because, on the one hand, the pathways of the disembodied souls, their planetary constellations, get attention. On the other hand, the reorganization takes place differently in the material cosmos, because the Christatmosphere was prepared by all the prophets of God so that the Kingdom of Peace can arise — of course, with a corresponding solar system and a planet Earth that does not correspond to the present one.

But all restructuring and transformation proceeds from the primordial central Being. The homebringing, that is, the guiding home of all souls and ensouled human beings, remains. This is guaranteed by the regency of the divine Wisdom, the third basic power of God.

The coming and going, above all, from the wheel of reincarnations, will be guided onto the appropriate pathways. In the knowledge of the massive global and cosmic changes on the Earth, as already reported, there will still be so-called Earth-spots, on which the restlessness and the all-too-human posturing wants to spread once again.

In the lower purification planes, which form a part of the wheel of reincarnations, souls will also live that want to try once more to build up their stronghold against God, which means: The demonic will rebel once more and cast a spell on many a one who believed they would be the Kingdom of Peace, themselves.

This twilight of the idols, which tries to spread here and there, comes from the remains of the Fall-system. Many a one from the church and state power, who, as a human being, was at the top of the spiritually criminal, believes as a soul that it needs to once again try for its power of authority. Via the wheel of reincarnations, as a human being he will then come to his kind on the Earth-spots that are still available for such souls — as a deterrent. Yet, it is done.

Therefore, there will still be times in which such attempts will be made. But during these times, the Earth will become ever more light-filled and finer, because a new heaven is announced, to which the corresponding planet belongs, which once carried this world. For more and more souls and human beings, this is a call to gradually follow the path to the eternal Father's house.

Thus, the ruler of the demonic regime has capitulated, even if many a human being, and later, many a soul, believes that they, indeed, still have to rebel.

It is finished. It is accomplished. It is done.

And the female being, called Satana, that wanted to be equal to the eternal Father-Mother-God and was abused and humiliated by the Satanist, the ruler of the Fall-system, for his Fall-purposes, will return to the Eternal Kingdom.

The Satanist's abuse of Satana's name, in order to humiliate the woman and to regard women merely as a means to an end right into this time — and this, under the secret of his personal disappointment and vanity — will continue to expose itself.

The former ruler of the Fall-realm is on his path of purification and many, indeed, very many, of his followers are with him. The souls in the lower purification planes, in the wheel of reincarnations, still believe in the so-called contingency of battle of wanting to eradicate everything. It will remain with wanting until insight is gained.

Everything is accomplished. It is done. The Kingdom of God is the victor in all the Fall-cosmoses and on the Earth on all the continents.

On the Earth and in the world, turbulences will continue to increase, because the karmic cortege, which is also called climate change, and of which the Eternal One revealed, moves on.

All over the Earth, on all continents, the cortege will point out the unatoned cruelties, also from past times.

The embodiments, the incarnations of human beings, or the souls on their wanderings will learn about and experience this, because the cortege of causalities justly brings everything to light.

Despite all this:
It is finished. It is accomplished. It is done.

Time moves on, the dawn, about which the eternal, All-One God revealed, brings forth the appearance of the Christ of God and a more light-filled planet, which was once called "Earth" and "world."

Dear fellow people, eternity has won. Spoken with our three-dimensional words: The capitulation of the head of the Fall-realm is completed. This has now been made known in the demonic state, also that the signet has been thrown onto the Earth as a sign of capitulation. This has caused and continues to cause more and more followers of the demonic state to desert.

As usual, those in solidarity come together to discuss how to proceed and whether they should follow their former ruler via the spheres of expiation.

It is as it is: The Eternal Kingdom leaves both human beings and soul beings their freedom. This is why the skirmishes will continue in the various countries in this world for a long time to come. But in all finer-material cosmoses, transformation is the order of the day.

From the Kingdom of God, more and more divine beings come to help all souls — no matter on which level of consciousness a soul is — and to answer their questions.

The path goes upward into the Eternal Kingdom, into the Father's house.

Every soul and every person is given the opportunity to walk this path, even if it might still be a long path of consciousness.

Dear fellow people, everything has been given to the people of this world, everything that was possible to be revealed in four thousand years with our three-dimensional words.

During nearly five decades, the cornucopia from the Sanctum of God was poured out once more. The Regent of the third basic power of God, the divine Wisdom, has summarized the eternal word of all God's messengers, of all men and women faithful to God of the past four thousand years, for all coming generations.

In the divine prophetic word through me, the emissary of God, he has given it again, in order to make it accessible to today's generations and future generations.

It can be read and heard in the *Tent of God Among the People,* in the shelter of the Eternal Word, in the *Ark of the Covenant of the Free Spirit.*

The Regent of the third basic power of God — as it was revealed to us human beings — was once the prophet Isaiah. As Regent of the third basic power, the eternal Wisdom, he has fulfilled his mission.

People, inspired by the Spirit of God, gradually bring the divine word back to the eternal All-One.

In this awareness and according to the will of the Eternal, I, Gabriele, the prophetess of God, in all humility and thankfulness, return His Holy Primordial Eternal Word in the prophetic existence to the sole Majesty of Infinity, the Father-Mother-God.

Eternal, All-One God, times ago, You asked me to take on Your eternal word in the prophetic mission, then, when the sons, who are in the mission, do not accept Your word, Your power and glory, to found the Kingdom of Peace, and give New Jerusalem a chance, also by fulfilling the instructions concerning the three filiation attributes in the Father-Mother-Principle of the Being.

Father, eternal God, almighty Father-Mother-God, in Your hands now lies the task that I may fulfill as Your emissary, which You have entrusted to me for the time being.

In view of the divine all-encompassing pictorial revelations to Your emissary of the eternal Kingdom of God, I know that many more brothers will serve You and Your Son as the pioneers of the New Era.

Until Your call resounds in the heart of Your daughter, "Come to Me," I will be Your emissary. Eternal All-One, You give me instructions on how it will proceed now, how the New Era can begin. You, Eternal One, and Your Son desire the beginning under the Sign of the Lily, Sophia, in the

Messianic, Sophianic Age, which will blossom first in the hearts of the people, the love for God and the love for neighbor. In the awareness of Your "Let there be," the Kingdom of Peace of Jesus Christ, New Jerusalem, will rise at the right time.

In this still harsh and cold world, as far as the eternal word from the Kingdom of God is concerned, I, Gabriele, will continue to work as Your emissary of the Kingdom of God for as long as You, O Eternal God, will it. Your will is done.

For the New Era, pioneers who fulfill the commandment of life will bring forward the foundation for the New Era, for a brighter time, as far as it is possible on the coarse-material Earth.

The mission of the Kingdom of Peace, the New Jerusalem, shines in many hearts of the pioneers for a more light-filled time. God, the Eternal, who has announced the transformation of the coarse-material, and also of the finer-material, that is, more light-filled, cosmoses, makes it come true. Pioneers, people vivified by

God, are with Him and His Son, the Co-Regent of the Kingdom of God.

I, Gabriele, am still a human being, but the homebringing and the leading home of all ensouled beings is in the mission of the regency of the third basic power of God, of His eternal Wisdom.

Dear brothers and sisters, spoken in working for the New Era:

At some point the call of the Almighty God will come to my soul and to me, the human being, Gabriele: *"Now it is time, come back to Me, to the eternal Father's House,"* thus, one thing is certain: When we no longer see each other from person to person, I stand in the divine mission, united with the Regent of God's third basic power and with many brothers and sisters who are still in the earthly garment, for the Age of the Lily and for building New Jerusalem.

United in eternal love,
Gabriele